Can We Know for Certain We Are
Going to Heaven?

Ralph O. Muncaster

HARVEST HOUSE PUBLISHERS
Eugene, OR 97402

Cover by Terry Dugan Design, Minneapolis, Minnesota

By Ralph O. Muncaster

Are There Hidden Codes in the Bible?
Can Archaeology Prove the New Testament?
Can Archaeology Prove the Old Testament?
Can We Know for Certain We Are Going to Heaven?
Can You Trust the Bible?
Creation vs. Evolution
Creation vs. Evolution Video
Does the Bible Predict the Future?
How to Talk About Jesus with the Skeptics in Your Life
How Do We Know Jesus Is God?
Is the Bible Really a Message from God?
Science—Was the Bible Ahead of Its Time?
What Is the Proof for the Resurrection?
What Really Happened Christmas Morning?
What Really Happens When You Die?
Why Does God Allow Suffering?

CAN WE KNOW FOR CERTAIN WE ARE GOING TO HEAVEN?
Examine the Evidence Series

Copyright © 2001 by Ralph O. Muncaster
Published by Harvest House Publishers
Eugene, Oregon 97402

Library of Congress Cataloging-in-Publication Data

Muncaster, Ralph O.
    Can we know for certain we are going to heaven? / Ralph O. Muncaster.
       p. cm. — (Examine the evidence series)
    Includes bibliographical references.
    ISBN 0-7369-0611-8
       1. Heaven. I. Title
BT846.3 .M86 2001
236'.24—dc21   00-047125

Printed in the United States of America.

01 02 03 04 05 06 07 08 09 / BP-GB / 10 9 8 7 6 5 4 3 2 1

Contents

Heaven—Real or Fantasy? How Do We Get There?

Death is certain.

Is heaven also certain? Is there an alternative to heaven, which some people call "hell"? These are vital questions—every human being should place the highest priority on examining them. After all, would you deliberately sail into an oncoming storm without being prepared? Would you face an impending hurricane without evaluating its effect and outcome? And if you knew a tornado were going to touch down in your neighborhood, would you think of risking your own life and the lives of your children and family by not preparing for it?

Death is more certain than anything else. Why don't people investigate it with the same intensity with which they investigate far less certain events, such as storms, hurricanes and tornados? After all, *physical death is permanent.*

Everyone wonders what lies beyond death. Most people believe in some kind of heaven or paradise, or in a process of reincarnation that ultimately results in a transcendent or "glorious" state. Some people believe that only a heaven exists, with no alternative such as hell. And some believe that there is nothing at all after death.

So a prudent person—one who acts upon the knowledge that death is certain—would 1) determine *whether there is* a heaven; 2) if it exists, discover *what is required* to attain it; and 3) take steps to *achieve* it.

This is simply common sense. But why do we spend so much time on our career, our vacation, our golf game, and other things when the issues of death and heaven lurk at our door? Whatever comes after death is *eternal.* Only a fool would trade away an eternity for a trifling temporary pleasure.

This book is designed to guide you in your investigation of heaven and the way you get there. The investigation is not difficult. But since we all, consciously or unconsciously, believe something about life after death, we must start out to gain a basis for what we believe.

The Key Issues

1. Does Heaven Exist?

If heaven doesn't exist, then it's a waste of time to determine how to get there. So as a first step, it's necessary to determine whether the existence of heaven is likely. (See pages 6–9, 34, 35.)

2. What Authority Can We Trust?

Where do we look to help us decide whether heaven is real? We must find an authority that can *prove* itself able to foretell things we don't know. Otherwise we're just guessing. (See pages 6–9.)

3. What Is Heaven Like?

What does this reliable authority tell us heaven is like? Are the popular ideas about heaven correct? Are all religions true? (See pages 10–12.)

4. What If We Don't Go to Heaven?

Consulting this reliable authority, what do we find happens to people who don't go to heaven? (See pages 13, 34, 35.)

5. How Do We Make Sure We Go to Heaven?

Assuming that heaven is real and that it is the place we desire to spend our eternity, how can we attain it? What do we have to do—believe something, or accept something? How can we know for certain? (See pages 14–47.)

Selecting the Authority for Our Beliefs About Heaven

How do we know what to believe about heaven? After all, virtually *all* religions claim they speak with authority about the afterlife; many speak about some form of "heaven." These religions usually revere a holy book as their final, authoritative source.

How do we know which guide is accurate, if any?

Look at it this way: Life after death is a supernatural event. Heaven—if it exists—is therefore a supernatural place. It exists beyond time and space in a dimension we can call the "spirit world." God also—if He exists—lives in the spirit world. Therefore, if God has provided information about life after death through a holy writing, we might expect to find evidence that this writing is from beyond time and space.

How Can We Know What Is from Beyond Time and Space?

"Miracle" is a word we use to describe something that is beyond our understanding, something that apparently has come from beyond time and space. We usually think of a miracle as an event—it might be a supernatural healing or some other happening that seems to defy the laws of physics. So how do we detect miracles in the written words of a text that is supposed to be authoritative?

Some religions maintain that the beauty of language in their holy text shows divine inspiration (for instance, Muslims believe this of the Qur'an). However, exceptional writers often demonstrate similar skill. Other groups point to supernatural events as the basis for belief that their holy books are inspired (for example, the giving of the "golden plates" containing the *Book of Mormon*). Yet no reasonable verification for these events exists.

The Bible displays several indications of supernatural, miraculous inspiration. First, its *authorship* is amazing. Written in various locations by at least 40 authors with different backgrounds over a period of 1500 years, the Bible is constant and internally consistent on hundreds of controversial topics.*

Second, the Bible also has a multitude of *concealed evidence* embedded in its pages. Numerical symbology, many models (or "types") and similitudes, and scientific insights are consistent throughout it; they tie centuries of writings together.†

And third, the Bible is miraculous in its *survival*. No other text has ever faced such intense efforts to eradicate it. Early Christians were often killed merely for the possession of a Bible—as are many Christians even today. And at the most extreme, in A.D. 303 the Roman emperor decreed the death penalty for anyone found with a Bible. Countless copies of the Bible were destroyed— yet the Bible still survived. In fact, today we have more ancient copies of the Bible—by far—than of any other ancient text.

But in spite of all the foregoing, there is only one sure test:

> The only certain test of God's inspiration of anything is— *perfect prediction of the future.*

And the only way we can verify this miracle of inspiration is to have *historical* prophecies contained in the text—prophecies about history that can be confirmed by actual later events. Predictions of end-time events are of no value in verifying a holy text because the events haven't happened yet—and therefore cannot be tested. But specific prophecies about historical people, places, or events can be used to confirm divine input in a holy writing.

Historical Prophecy in the Bible

The Bible is unique, in that it consistently foretells the future with absolute accuracy. Consider the fact that the Bible contains over 600 specific historical prophecies—with not one wrong. Most other holy books are totally void of historical prophecy. The test of anything being "from God" is prophecy (Deuteronomy

---

* See *Is the Bible Really a Message from God?* in the *Examine the Evidence* series.

† See *Does the Bible Contain Hidden Codes?* in the *Examine the Evidence* series.

18:17-22; Isaiah 46:10). The Bible was written over a period of 1500 years; we can trust the generations who came after the times of the prophecies to be honest about the historical facts, since they would have had no motive to conceal errors. These generations saw many specific historical events that confirmed the prophecies of the Bible.

Summary of the Accuracy of Biblical Prophecy[1]

	Old Testament Prophecies	New Testament Prophecies	Total	% of Total
Historically fulfilled	467	201	668	68%
Fulfillment not confirmed	2*	1*	3*	<1%
Heaven or the future (to be fulfilled)	105	237	342	32%
Total	574	439	1013	100%

* Prophecies whose fulfillment is not verified: Jeremiah 35:1-19; 49:1-6; John 1:49-51.

Prophecy in Other Holy Books

The holy books of world religions contain virtually no verifiable historical prophecy. Some contain end-of-time prophecies that cannot be proven until the end of time—which does us no good as a test. Prophetic analysis of some of these holy books follows:

Failed Prophecies of Mormon Holy Books

The Book of Mormon—The following prophecy was written in 1823, long after Jesus was born: Jesus "shall be born . . . at Jerusalem" (Alma 7:10). He was actually born in Bethlehem. Some Mormons say Bethlehem was a part of Jerusalem, being only five miles away. Yet five miles at that time required more than an hour's travel—much like a 60-mile commute today. Even now,

Bethlehem is considered a separate city from Jerusalem. This after-the-fact prophecy is false.

Doctrines and Covenants (D&C)—This book prophesied in 1832 that a temple and a new Jerusalem would be built at a specific site in west Missouri within a generation (D&C 84:1-5,31). It was again emphasized in 1833 (D&C 97:19) and later (D&C 101:17-21) that the new Jerusalem would *never* be moved from Missouri. Yet Salt Lake City became the "Jerusalem," and many generations have passed with no temple ever built in Missouri. These prophecies are false.

Failed Prophecies of the Jehovah's Witnesses

Various Publications—Many prophecies declaring the end of the world have been published by the Jehovah's Witnesses. The predictions mention these years: 1874 (*Studies in the Scriptures* 7:301); 1914 (same, 2:101); 1915 (same, 1914 edition); 1918 (same, 7:62); 1920 (same, 7:542); 1925 (*Millions Now Living Will Never Die*, Rutherford, 1920, page 97); 1942 (*The New World*, Rutherford, 1942, page 104); and 1975 (*Kingdom Ministry*, March 1968, page 4). Obviously, all such attempts at prophecy have failed.

**Conclusion: The Bible is the only source
with 100-percent prophetic accuracy—
and therefore is the only reliable authority on heaven.**

What Heaven Is Like

Virtually all cultures have some concept of heaven. Yet none of these other concepts is supported by the evidence in the way the Bible is (see pages 6–9).

Heaven Described

Heaven is beyond imagining—beyond all description. Jesus proclaimed that heaven would be worth trading everything for (Matthew 13:44-46). But the most complete description of heaven is in the book of Revelation. Keep in mind that John, the author of Revelation, was shown many things that are totally unlike anything here on earth. Consequently, he had to express heaven's beauty in terms of the earthly beauty that was familiar to him and his readers.

While we can't experience or even truly imagine the wonder of heaven until we arrive, we can trust the words of Jesus that heaven is worth more than anything.

Heaven and Earth Today . . . A New Heaven and Earth Tomorrow

Heaven today is the abode of God, of the spirits of people who have accepted Jesus, and of the angels that serve God. Only spirits now exist in heaven—spirits without bodies. After the second coming of Jesus, the spirits of people in heaven will be reunited with their new glorified bodies (2 Corinthians 5:4,5; Revelation 20:4), and God's people will enjoy a new, "heavenly" earth with no more tears, suffering, or death (Revelation 21:4).

The Bible makes a distinction between the heaven of today and the new heaven and the new earth to come (Revelation 21:1). Earth is for bodies united with spirits. Heaven today is for spirits only. But in eternity, everyone will be united with a body—whether a glorious, indestructible one in heaven, or one subject to eternal torment in hell. And God will reside with believers for eternity on the new earth (Revelation 21:3).

The new earth, specifically the holy city (the new Jerusalem) is

What Does Heaven Look Like?

The throne: God is on it. It has the appearance of jasper* and carnelian. There are blazes of lightning and thunder.

The rainbow around the throne: "like an emerald" (Revelation 4:3).

The 24 elders around the throne: They are dressed in white with crowns on their heads. Perhaps they are the leaders of the 12 tribes of Israel and the 12 apostles.

The sea of glass**: In front of the throne—"like crystal."

The glorious creatures: Four of them surround the throne. Each has six wings and many eyes covering them. They have the heads of a lion, an ox, a man, and an eagle.***

What Do We Do In Heaven?

Worship: It will be a great and everlasting spiritual thrill to worship the one almighty God in heaven.

Enjoy God: For the first time since Adam, God will truly exist with humankind (Revelation 21:4).

Enjoy other people: Believers will live with other believers, including family and friends.

Have no sorrow, ever: No more death, no more mourning, no more sadness— forever.

Be filled with delight: Incredible heavenly golf courses? Symphonies beyond description? We can only imagine it in terms of the best of earth. God promises us eternal pleasure (Psalm 16:11).

(See Revelation 4,20,21)

* Jasper, at the time of Christ, was the name for diamond.

** Perfectly refined gold is clear like glass.

*** Lion=king, ox=slave, man=man, eagle=God. These are the primary roles of Jesus that are reflected in the Gospels.

described in glorious terms. It will shine in the brilliance of the light emanating from God Himself (Revelation 21:11). It will have walls of jasper—diamond (21:18), streets of pure gold (transparent), and gates of pearl (21:21). Very significantly, it will contain the "tree of life" mentioned at the beginning, at the time of the great separation of mankind from God (Genesis 3:22,23). There will no longer be any curse against man or upon the earth (Revelation 22:3). And the throne of God will be the throne of both God and Jesus, the Lamb (the remover of the curse through His sacrifice on the cross—see 22:1).

What Hell Is Like

Hell (Gehenna), just like heaven, is also beyond description, and there is no place on earth that compares to it. Jesus used the word "Gehenna" because it was the most relevant term for the Jews of His time.

The Horror of Hell

Gehenna is an actual place in the Hinnom Valley just southwest of Jerusalem. King Solomon, in his later years, turned the valley from a natural paradise into a place where the idols of his wives' pagan gods were worshipped. Infants were sacrificed into terrifying flames. The valley later became the city cesspool where refuse, dead animals, and bodies of criminals were dumped and burned. Worms ate into dead flesh until they were consumed by the blaze. The fires never ceased. The foul stench never stopped. To the Jews, Gehenna was absolute hell.

The Bible describes hell several times as a place where "the fire never goes out" (for example, in Mark 9:43), where a lake of fire burns with sulfur (Revelation 19:20), and where worms never die (Mark 9:47,48).

The darkness of hell is complete. Since the only light at the end of time, in heaven, will be from God and Jesus (Revelation 21:23-25; 22:5), hell will be eternal darkness—a place where everyone and everything is separated from God forever (Matthew 8:12; 22:13; 25:30).

Jesus used the earthly horror of Gehenna to give us an idea of the horror of hell. Jesus never minced words. He was direct. Hell is horrible. Jesus described hell several times as the place where there will be "weeping and gnashing of teeth" (Matthew 8:12; 22:13; 24:51; 25:30).

> While it's difficult to know exactly what hell is, we can be certain it is a terrible place that everyone would want to avoid.

Getting to Heaven:

What Do We Believe About God and Jesus?

"Without faith it is impossible to please God,
because anyone who comes to him must *believe that he exists*
and that he *rewards those who earnestly seek him.*
—Hebrews 11:6

If you want to come to God, it is a requirement first of all that you believe He exists. And if you come to believe what the Bible says about God, you will also come to believe what it says about Jesus. In other words, if you seek God through the Bible, you will find Jesus—because the Bible is from God, and Jesus is God. The Bible's origin from God is demonstrated by its miraculous prophecy, its historical accuracy (as verified by archaeology), and by many other points of evidence that compel us to believe what it says about Jesus and His fulfillment of historical prophecies. (This is the basic premise of the *Examine the Evidence* series.)

How could anyone accept Jesus as God's gift unless that person came to believe these things about Him?

1. He was an actual person who lived on earth.

2. He was born from a woman who was a virgin, which is proof that He is both God and man.

3. He was crucified as a sacrifice for the sins of human beings.

4. He rose from the dead, which proves His deity and His triumph over evil.

All of these points should be simple to believe once the evidence has been investigated. (Note that Hebrews 11:6 declares that God *rewards those who earnestly seek Him.* Any research or investigation will not be in vain.)

1. Did Jesus exist?

There is more evidence of Jesus' existence than that of any other person from ancient times. Along with supporting archaeological finds, there are more than 24,000 existing early manuscripts of Scripture. All of this testifies to the fact that His existence was unquestioned among the people of His time.[2,3,4,5]

2. Was He born from a woman who was a virgin, which displayed both His deity and His humanity?

The Old Testament stated, in a dual prophecy, that "the Lord himself will give you a sign: The virgin...will give birth to a son, and they will call him Immanuel" (Isaiah 7:14). "Immanuel" means "God with us," identifying precisely who God intended Jesus to be. Textual and linguistic research also clearly indicates that the texts in Isaiah and Matthew (1:23) are speaking of a virgin, not just a young woman. Furthermore, widespread belief in Jesus' virgin birth, both before and during Jesus' time, is evidenced by writings in the Jewish Talmud that indirectly attack this belief.

3 & 4. Was He crucified as a sacrifice and raised from the dead?

The Hebrew Scriptures (the Old Testament) prefigured these events in many places (Psalm 22, Isaiah 53, and others). Jesus' death and His resurrection were prophesied by Jesus Himself at least three times; the fulfillment of these prophecies was necessary to show that He was a prophet from God—100-percent accurate in what He predicted. Therefore, Jesus' declarations that He was God can be trusted as well (Mark 14:61-63; John 5:16-27; 10:30-38).

The evidence that confirms and supports these events is overwhelming: the existence of the Christian church today, which is based on these historical facts; the records written by non-Christians; the supporting findings from archaeological research; and more.[2,3,4,5,6,7]

The life, death, and resurrection of Jesus, grounded in historical fact, make a bridge between the seen and the unseen. The evidence about Jesus helps support faith, which is being "certain of what we do not see" (Hebrews 11:1). Faith is the only way to have a relationship with God.

Getting to Heaven:
Commitment to Jesus

"Others, like seed sown on good soil, *hear the word,
accept it,* and produce a crop—thirty, sixty or even
a hundred times what was sown."
—*Jesus, in Mark 4:20*

"Still you people [the religious leaders] *do not accept* our testimony.
I have spoken to you of earthly things and you do not believe [or
accept]; how then will you believe if I speak of heavenly things?"
—*Jesus, in John 3:11,12*

Belief deals with the intellectual knowledge that Jesus existed,
that He was God in human form, and that His fundamental role
on earth was to die and be raised from the dead as an eternal
sacrifice for all who accept Him. *Acceptance* means a commitment
in three key things that are all interdependent:

Decision: Commitment		
Acceptance of Jesus' sacrifice	Repentance from sin	Making Jesus Lord

Note that the key element in assuring heaven is a commitment
to God by acknowledging His love expressed through Jesus. It
involves the three inseparable elements shown above:

- *Accepting God's gift of Jesus*—forgiveness from an imperfect
  life, recognizing that the sacrifice of Jesus on the cross is the
  only way to obtain that forgiveness.
- *Repenting*—turning away from the evil of your past life.
- *Making Jesus the Lord of your life*—so that He will direct your
  decisions from this point forward.

**Acceptance, Repentance, and Lordship are
interdependent and inseparable.**

How could we truly accept the gift of forgiveness through the
enormous, loving sacrifice of Jesus without making Him Lord?

And how could we make Him Lord without repenting of our sin as He commanded? All these things come together as a whole.

Why is acceptance so important? Suppose someone mailed you a gift of a million dollars. You *knew* the person mailed it. You *believed* it when you saw the box delivered by the mailman. But you *didn't accept* the box. You didn't open it. How would you ever gain the benefits of the gift? What would your refusal say about you?

When it comes to the acceptance of Jesus, the stakes are infinitely higher. God did everything to provide what we need to come to Him. He even came to earth, sacrificed Himself (in the person of Jesus) in human form by the most painful death ever invented, and then provided everyone the gift of forgiveness—just for the asking. Furthermore, God has provided extensive evidence that He is real and that His means of forgiveness and getting to heaven are real.

Think of it. When people "turn away the mailman," they are refusing a great gift that they could investigate to substantiate its truthfulness. Refusing to accept the great gift of forgiveness God has provided is essentially "thumbing our nose" at God. It's like saying, "I really don't want your gift." When this is done throughout one's

Do Satan and the Demons Believe?

The Bible tells us that Satan and his demons believe the facts about Jesus (James 2:19). They know He is the Son of God. Matthew 8:28-34 speaks of demons that clearly knew that Jesus was the Son of God. It's also clear they knew the final outcome—that they would be cast into hell at the end of time ("Have you come here to torture us before the appointed time?"—verse 29).

This demonstrates the huge difference between intellectual belief and acceptance. The demons believed, but they certainly didn't accept Jesus as their Lord and Savior.

life, despite knowledge of the truth and prompting by the Holy Spirit, it's called "blasphemy of the Holy Spirit"—the one unforgivable sin (Matthew 12:31).

The acceptance of Jesus must be a conscious, willful decision by an individual. It is an individual's heart that God is seeking (see pages 21–23). There is no substitute for acceptance. Not church attendance. Not great community service. Not prayer. *Nothing can substitute for the acceptance of Jesus*—our returning to God the love that He has shown us all.

Getting to Heaven:

Repentance

"Jesus began to preach,
'Repent, for the kingdom of heaven is near.'"
—*Matthew 4:17*

"As for you, you were dead in your transgressions
and sins, in which you used to live when you
followed the ways of this world."
—*Ephesians 2:1,2*

Repentance simply means "turning away" from sin and one's
former life. It includes a sincere desire to follow Jesus. We can
repent in the instant we commit to Jesus, because it involves a
basic desire to live differently (2 Peter 3:9). If we have truly
accepted Jesus, the Holy Spirit will be in us, working out our
new desire to change and also subconsciously telling us when we
are doing wrong. No one has to be perfect on earth to get to heaven.
That's what the sacrifice of Jesus was all about. God's grace is
enough to overcome all our weaknesses (2 Corinthians 12:9).

Though repentance
is instant, change doesn't
happen overnight!

People should never expect a "bolt of lightning"—that upon
accepting Jesus, they will begin consistently living the way He
taught. All people go on sinning in some form and to some
degree. But a new life in Jesus changes the way we think. Sin
becomes less attractive; conviction comes from the Holy Spirit
helping us to realize what is sin; and we learn to be confident
that God has granted us forgiveness through Jesus. The Holy
Spirit residing in us will also give us assurance that we are God's
children (Romans 8:15,16). If these things are not the case, then
we should consider again our acceptance of Jesus. In short:

Sin lessens over time. Goodness increases.
and
God's grace, not your perfection, is the key to heaven.

Eventually, God will produce good in our lives (Philippians 1:6). The following "fruit" is evidence of His work:

Love, joy, peace, patience, kindness, goodness, faithfulness, gentleness, and self-control (see Galatians 5:22,23).

We all should expect the "fruit" above. If after a long time nothing has changed, acceptance, repentance, and lordship should be considered again.

Getting to Heaven:

Lordship

"If you love me, you will obey what I command."
—*Jesus, in John 14:15*

"If you obey my commands, you will remain
in my love, just as I have obeyed my Father's
commands and remain in his love."
—*Jesus, in John 15:10*

For many people, the most difficult part of the commitment to Jesus that ensures a place in heaven is this: giving Jesus lordship over their lives. Lordship means turning one's life over to the will of God through Jesus. This commitment to "ownership" by God will be lived out by asking God about decisions and following the Holy Spirit's promptings, which often come through the words of the Bible or through other Christians. Such a commitment to God's control seems completely at odds with people's natural desire to run their own lives; it seems as though it would radically interfere with doing "what they really want to do."

This would in fact be the case, except for this—commitment to Jesus brings a new life into a person's heart, a life that *wants* to love God and follow Jesus. A person cannot accept Jesus' lordship without also accepting Jesus' love, and vice versa (see the verses above). This love changes us so that we desire to follow His commands; we want to follow God's will.

Hence, if someone is following a Jesus who is not real, that person will not experience God's love. He or she is making a false idea lord, rather than embracing the Lord of lords. Jesus said, "Not everyone who says to me, 'Lord, Lord,' will enter the kingdom of heaven" (Matthew 7:21). Jesus would not "know" a person who made a false Jesus his or her Lord (such as followers of various religions that call themselves Christian: for example, Christian Scientists, Mormons, and Jehovah's Witnesses—see insert about "know" on page 22).

Furthermore, some people think that following a lot of religious rules and merely calling Jesus "Lord" will get them to heaven, even though they have never committed themselves to the real Jesus, God's Son. Jesus spoke about such people: "I will tell them plainly, '*I never knew you*. Away from me, you evildoers!'" (Matthew 7:23.

Summary

It is critical to *commit* to Jesus, which encompasses three inseparable things: accepting Him as God's sacrifice so we can be forgiven, repenting from our former lives, and embracing Him as Lord. Mere assent to the facts about Him, mere belief of ideas about Him, demeans His deity. It mocks His loving sacrifice—the most loving thing anyone could do for another human being, which is to die in his or her place. Since Jesus is who He said He is—God in human flesh—He deserves our commitment. And our commitment to Him as Savior and Lord is the wisest and best course for us. After all, who would know better how to guide us than the One who created us?

What Does "Believe" or "Know" Really Mean?

"...Whoever believes in him [Jesus] shall not perish but have eternal life" (John 3:16). Some people might think from reading this that a mere intellectual belief in Jesus will get them to heaven. This is not so (for instance, the demons, who are doomed to hell, believe the facts about Jesus—see the insert on page 17). The Greek word translated "believe" is *pisteuo*, which carries the sense of "put one's trust in."[8]

Likewise, the word for "know" used in Matthew 7:23 (the Greek word *ginosko*) implies "completely understand" or "have an active connection with"—in other words, a *relationship*—something that goes far beyond just assenting to facts.

Therefore, to *believe in* Jesus is to *put your trust* in Him. To *know* Jesus is to *have a relationship* with Him.

Getting to heaven is straightforward, simple, and free, once we realize that it demands *everything* of us. Having established an intellectual belief that Jesus is real, that He walked on this earth, and that He was crucified for our sin and was resurrected, we then commit ourselves to Him (see previous page). The result of this commitment is a new life for us—an inward transformation (2 Corinthians 5:17). We are freed from the guilt of the past and have a Guide for the future. We begin to produce "good fruit."

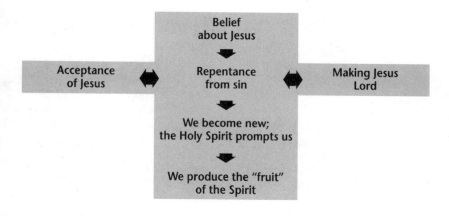

The Pathway to Heaven...

Heaven
(a spiritual abode with God)

The Spirit
Leaves the Body

Those
who have
accepted
Jesus

Those
who
reject
Jesus

"Un-
knowers" of
Jesus (?)

SOMETIME IN

The spirit is
reunited
with the body

The Great Tribulation

New Heaven

New Earth

The 1000-Year Reign of Christ

Those who accepted Jesus

(Eternal Paradise)

The Judgment at the White Throne

Facts—What the Bible Says Is Required to Get to Heaven

- *Belief* that the Jesus of the Bible came to earth and is the Son of God—God in human flesh—and that He came to be a perfect sacrifice for our sin (see pages 14, 15).
- *Acceptance* of the gift of the Son, recognizing God as the provider (see pages 16–18).
- *Switching* from our former life—that is, repentance (see pages 19, 20).
- *Expressly making Jesus Christ our Lord*—the One who directs our lives (see pages 21–23).

...How to Be Certain[5]

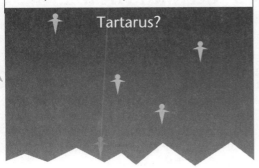

Sheol-Hades
(a place of the spirits of the dead)

Tartarus?

Great Chasm

Place of Comfort—"Abraham's Bosom"
(if still in existence)

THE FUTURE

The spirit is
reunited with
the body

Those who did not accept Jesus

Hell
(Gehenna, the Lake of Fire)

Myths About How to Get to Heaven

- *Be good* so that we can "earn" our way to heaven. Only Jesus is the way to heaven—and He must be accepted as a *gift*. Only He is perfect. Nothing else, no one else is good enough for God (see pages 26, 27).

- *Attend church.* Merely being in a building, or meeting with other people, will do nothing for you. You must have the right *relationship* with God through Jesus (see page 27).

The faithful people of the Old Testament and (perhaps) "Un-knowers" of Jesus

- *Serve others.* Though it may help other people, it does nothing to bring us into a *relationship* with God, which is the only way to get to heaven. Many people do good things for others but still reject God (see pages 27, 28).

- *Pray.* Prayer to the wrong god, or prayer to the real God when we don't know Him through Jesus, gets us nowhere.

Common Misconceptions About Getting to Heaven

1. Being "Good" Gets Me to Heaven

Unfortunately, most people who expect to go to heaven expect to do so on the basis of their "goodness" on earth. This is not what the Bible says. Before anything, we need to realize we are subject to a perfectly holy God. What we, in our very limited human view, think of as "good" is not good in God's sight. For example, the "heroes of the Bible" were heroes not because they were "good" (in fact, some of them committed heinous crimes), but because they believed what God said and had a relationship with Him. God forgave them, just as He will forgive us, *only through His grace,* poured out because of the ultimate sacrifice of Jesus.

One of the most notable heroes of all is Saul (who became Paul). Saul was one of the greatest persecutors of Christians (Acts 7:58; 9:1,2). Yet once he experienced the risen Jesus and His love (Acts 9), he totally changed. Did Paul believe in the resurrection, even though he had previously been rounding up Christians for torture and death? Yes! And then he committed his life to Jesus.

Knowing that he was completely loved and forgiven, Paul gave up position—he went from being a prestigious Pharisee to an outcast Christian. He left wealth and security and then endured incredible suffering: relentless treks to spread the gospel, torture, stoning, imprisonment, and shipwreck. In spite of his evil acts before accepting Jesus, he wrote more of the books of the New Testament than anyone—books about Jesus. He started more major early churches of Christians than anyone else. Paul realized that "being good" doesn't get people to heaven—only God's grace does, through our acceptance of Jesus' sacrifice. Paul and his fellow apostle Peter said:

> "It is *by grace* you have been saved, *through faith*—
> and this *not from yourselves,* it is the gift of God—
> not by works, so that no one can boast."
> —*Ephesians 2:8,9*

"It is through the *grace* of our Lord Jesus that we are saved."
—*Acts 15:11*

Bottom Line: No one is perfectly "good." Even if we think we don't sin through our actions, we certainly sin with our thoughts (Matthew 5:27,28). Therefore, no one is good enough to get to heaven on his or her own. Committing ourselves to Jesus (see pages 16–23)—establishing a relationship with Him—will allow *God* to make us good. Only Jesus' goodness is "good enough" to get us to heaven; and His goodness is a gift from God that comes with forgiveness and new life. This is God's grace—our key to heaven. "Grace and truth came through Jesus Christ" (John 1:17).

To put it in a different light, God's plan for us requires that we have a redeemer (someone who "buys us back" out of our slavery to sin and evil). The only redeemer who is good enough in the sight of a perfectly holy God to "pay the cost" to buy us back is—again—Jesus, who is God Himself in human form. And it is, once more, through Jesus that we are "made perfect"—perfect enough for heaven (Hebrews 10:10,14).

2. Going to Church Gets Me to Heaven

Some people believe that going to church a few times a year, or more often, is a way to ensure getting to heaven. The Bible doesn't teach this. As the Holy Spirit works on a new believer's heart, that person will *want* to meet with other believers, often in a church. But simply going into a church building does nothing to get a person to heaven—only Jesus can do that. God is interested in each individual's personal relationship with Him, not some rote activity. Go to church because you are responding to God's love through Jesus, not because you feel you have to in order to "earn" heaven.

3. Serving Others Gets Me to Heaven

Virtually no religion would denounce service to other people. But the Bible does not say that serving others has anything to do with gaining entrance into heaven. Many people who strongly reject God are very "good" people (from the human standpoint)—they are often philanthropists and serve others in many ways. But would God offer an eternity in His presence to people who reject Him, His love, and the sacrifice of His Son Jesus, while they take pride and find glory in their "service"? As Jesus said, such people have already "received their reward in full" here on earth (Matthew 6:1-4); they cannot gain heaven by their "good acts."

Jesus spoke often about the importance of being a servant, but always with the understanding that He and His mission would be believed and accepted first. When a person accepts Jesus, repents, and makes Him Lord, the desire to serve other people will increase. This is because a person who commits to Jesus receives the life of Jesus—and Jesus Himself is both a servant and the ultimate model of a servant (Philippians 2:3-7). His will and His desire are a believer's reason to serve. The motivation is not one's own desire to be applauded. The point is, serving others isn't a key to heaven; it's a *result* of loving God because of His giving heaven to us through His Son.

4. Following Church Rules Gets Me to Heaven

Many churches have certain rules or expected procedures for their members. Some of these rules are beneficial, others are not. But in regard to gaining heaven, God doesn't make "rule-following" a requirement. In fact, Jesus criticized "rules taught by men" (Matthew 15:8,9). Why? Because each person's decision to commit to Jesus is a *personal* decision. A commitment made only to comply with church rules, not made from the heart, will be "in vain" (verse 9) because it is not a commitment to Jesus Himself. Rule-following will never bring us to heaven because no one reaches the Father except by way of Jesus, the Son. (This is not to suggest that church order is not important. In fact, much of the New Testament deals with believers' conduct in the church.) But don't fall into a trap of legalism, presuming that rules or traditions will get you into heaven or keep you out. Such ideas are not biblically based.

5. Everybody Gets into Heaven

Some religions teach that there is essentially no hell, and that nearly everyone gets into heaven (for example, Christian Scientists, Mormons to an extent, and many others). Some nonreligious people, reasoning from a human point of view, think that a God who is loving couldn't possibly send anyone to Hell.[5,9,10] The Bible, the only trustworthy authority, clearly presents Jesus as the only way to heaven (see pages 30–35). Anyone who chooses to reject Him chooses hell. The Bible teaches that hell exists and is horrible, and that there will be a separation made between those who go to heaven and those who go to hell (Matthew 25:41; 2 Thessalonians 1:7-9; Revelation 20:10-15).

Doesn't the Bible Teach Goodness, Church Participation, and Service?

The Bible stresses all three of these things as important. This is one reason why people mistake them as ways to get to heaven.

The difference between popular misconceptions and the Bible's teaching is one of "cause" and "effect." If people think they can earn the way to heaven (be the "cause"), they are mistaken (see Ephesians 2:8,9 on page 26). On the other hand, when people realize that they first need to commit to Jesus as their Lord and Savior (He being the "cause"), and that they will then begin to produce "fruit" (the effect) because of God's grace and the Holy Spirit, this agrees completely with biblical teaching. The *relationship with Jesus* is the key to everything.

Jesus Is the Only Way to Heaven

Jesus Speaks About Himself

"Trust in God; trust also in me. In my Father's
house there are many rooms....
I am going there to prepare a place for you."
—John 14:1,2

"I am the way and the truth and the life.
No one comes to the Father except through me.
If you really knew me,
you would know my Father as well.
From now on, you do know him and *have seen* him."
—John 14:6,7

"I and the Father are one."
—John 10:30

The Bible has established itself as the only authority on the
supernatural (see pages 6–9) because only it has predicted the
future with 100-percent accuracy. And it is the Bible that records
the words of Jesus above—His claim that He is God *in human
flesh*. (There are also other places in Scripture where Jesus makes
this claim.)

Jesus' perfectly-fulfilled prophecy of
His death and resurrection confirmed
that He was and is God—
just as the Hebrew Scriptures
(the Old Testament)
had prophesied long before.

Jesus also declared that He has the authority to execute final
judgment upon human beings. He will separate those people
who will enter heaven from those who will not (Matthew
7:21-23; 25:31-46). His standard of judgment will require that
people *know* Him (see insert on page 22).

The Relationship of God to Jesus—
A Comparison of the Old Testament
with the New Testament[10]

"...There is but one God, the Father,
from whom all things came and for whom we live;
and there is but one Lord, Jesus Christ,
through whom all things came and through whom we live."
—*1 Corinthians 8:6*

The Old Testament describes God as...		The New Testament describes Jesus as...	
Creator	Genesis 1:1	**Creator**	John 1:1-3
	Job 33:4		Colossians 1:13-17
	Isaiah 40:28		Hebrews 1:8-12
First and Last	Isaiah 41:4	**First and Last**	Revelation 1:17
	Isaiah 44:6		Revelation 2:8
	Isaiah 48:12		Revelation 22:13
Judge	Genesis 18:25	**Judge**	2 Timothy 4:1
	Psalm 96:13		2 Corinthians 5:10
	Joel 3:12		Romans 14:10-12
King	Psalm 47	**King**	Matthew 2:3-6
	Isaiah 44:6		John 18:33-37
	Jeremiah 10:10		Revelation 19:11-16
Light	Psalm 27:1	**Light**	John 1:4-9
	Isaiah 60:20		John 8:12
Savior	Psalm 106:21	**Savior**	John 4:42
	Isaiah 43:3,11		Acts 4:10-12
	Isaiah 45:21		1 John 4:14
Shepherd	Psalm 23	**Shepherd**	John 10:11
	Psalm 100:3		Hebrews 13:20
	Isaiah 40:11		1 Peter 5:4

Why Is Jesus the Only Way to Heaven?

People often wonder, "Why is Jesus the only way? Why can't other religious beliefs be true too? Is the road to heaven really that narrow?" The Bible says it is:

> "Someone asked him [Jesus], 'Lord, are only
> a few people going to be saved?'
> He said to them, 'Make every effort to enter
> through the *narrow door*,
> because many, I tell you, will try to enter
> and will not be able to.' "
> —*Luke 13:23,24*

Jesus went on to explain that at some point the opportunity to enter will be closed, and many will then plead to get in, but God will turn them away because He never knew them (see page 22 for a clarification of "knew").

In talking about the "narrow road" to heaven, Jesus also warned of many "false prophets" who are like "ferocious wolves" (Matthew 7:14,15). False prophets and false religions will take you off the road to heaven. Any writing, religion, or person who can't be tested and verified by 100-percent accurate prophecy should be suspect.

It is vital to test our beliefs. The Bible is the only holy book that commands us to test everything (1 Thessalonians 5:21)—which includes testing the Bible itself. And the test that God has set up to help us verify whether something is from Him is the test of perfect prophecy (Deuteronomy 18:14-22; Isaiah 46:10). Testing prophecy is emphasized throughout the Bible—which is a book that itself contains more than 600 specific, historically fulfilled prophecies (see pages 6–9). No other person or book passes this test.

So when the Bible proclaims Jesus to be the only way (see page 30)—and since Jesus Himself declared that He was God and proved it through His perfect prophecy and through His resurrection from the dead—we can be confident that He is in fact the only way to heaven (John 3:16-18; 14:6).

How Does Jesus Fit into God's Plan for Human Beings?

The Bible makes it clear that God is perfectly
holy, loving, and just (see pages 34, 35).

Heaven must be perfectly *holy*, because it is the dwelling place of God. And God wants people with Him for eternity (Revelation 21:1-3). But no human being is perfectly holy. So God provided a solution to the problem; a way for people to become holy through complete forgiveness and redemption by a perfect sacrifice—His Son, Jesus (1 John 4:17-19). However, in order to gain this forgiveness and redemption, people need to accept God's gift of Jesus (see pages 16–23).

God's perfect *love* is demonstrated by 1) God's gift of free choice to humans—especially the choice to love Him[9]—and 2) His freely given gift of forgiveness through the sacrifice of Jesus. God showed His perfect love—as a Father, He gave up His only beloved Son by allowing Him to undergo the most horrible execution known to man. This displays God's incredible love for people—even for those who are His enemies. God wants human beings to love, worship, and enjoy Him in heaven, but this demands a choice to love Him. In this case, the choice to love God means accepting the loving sacrifice of Jesus. Nonacceptance is rejection of God's love.

Perfect *justice* is fulfilled by God's requirement that sin be punished. People can either choose to accept Jesus, who was sacrificed for sin in our place; or they can choose to bear the penalty themselves by rejecting God's love forever, despite the prompting of the Holy Spirit, and suffering eternal banishment to hell (Luke 12:4-10).

Why God Created...

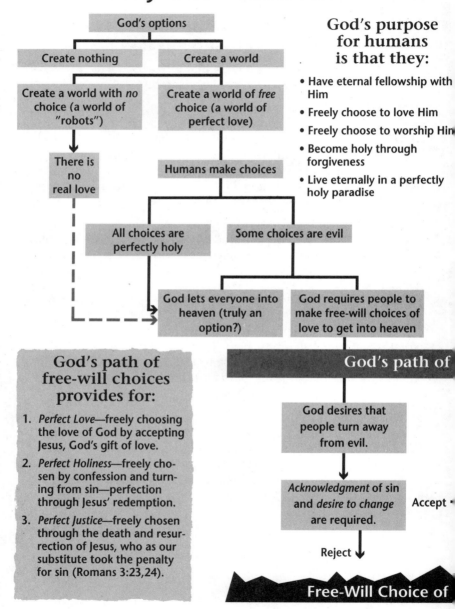

God's options

Create nothing

Create a world

Create a world with *no* choice (a world of "robots")

Create a world of *free* choice (a world of perfect love)

There is no real love

Humans make choices

God's purpose for humans is that they:

- Have eternal fellowship with Him
- Freely choose to love Him
- Freely choose to worship Him
- Become holy through forgiveness
- Live eternally in a perfectly holy paradise

All choices are perfectly holy

Some choices are evil

God lets everyone into heaven (truly an option?)

God requires people to make free-will choices of love to get into heaven

God's path of free-will choices provides for:

1. *Perfect Love*—freely choosing the love of God by accepting Jesus, God's gift of love.
2. *Perfect Holiness*—freely chosen by confession and turning from sin—perfection through Jesus' redemption.
3. *Perfect Justice*—freely chosen through the death and resurrection of Jesus, who as our substitute took the penalty for sin (Romans 3:23,24).

God's path of

God desires that people turn away from evil.

Acknowledgment of sin and *desire to change* are required.

Accept

Reject

Free-Will Choice of

...a Narrow Path to Heaven

Why this world is the *best solution* to achieve God's purposes:

1. God wants fellowship with human beings who love Him, so it was necessary for Him to make a world in which people could live, be given the choice to love Him, and be given the opportunity to develop holy character.

2. God wants humans to love Him perfectly. His desire made it necessary that He create a world of totally free choice.

3. The free choice that God granted to human beings also allows them to use His perfect creation for evil. Humans made the choice of evil in the beginning, though they may still turn from evil and choose the good.

4. God has provided a means for imperfect humans to choose to love Him and be forgiven for their past evil. The means He provided for forgiveness were the sacrifice of Himself in the person of His Son, Jesus.

5. Those people who do not accept Jesus' perfect sacrifice and His resurrection (which proves His deity) reject God's love, reject God's forgiveness, and reject Jesus—God—as Lord. Essentially they show disdain, not love, for God.

6. So this world of good and evil is essentially a sorting ground to determine who will choose to seek holiness and love God by freely accepting His gift of forgiveness—by accepting Jesus as *Lord* and *Savior*.

Free-will choices

God desires that all people be saved
(1 Timothy 2:3,4)—
that is, accept forgiveness—
and that they freely love Him as Lord
(Mark 12:30).

↓

Jesus was provided as the perfect sacrifice;
God then raised Him from the dead,
verifying His deity. He can be our
Savior and Lord.

Reject ↓

Heaven
Believers can perfectly experience their God-granted holiness and justification (Romans 3:23,24) and are completely free to express perfect love.

Accept →

Eternal Separation from God

What Is Eternal Salvation?

Webster's dictionary defines salvation as 1) "Preservation or deliverance from danger, evil or difficulty"; or 2) "Deliverance from the power or penalty of sin: REDEMPTION."

The Old Testament describes salvation largely in terms of the first definition. "Salvation" or "save" is used of Israel's deliverance from Egypt (Exodus 14:13; 15:2), from exile in Babylon (Isaiah 46:13; 52:10,11), from adversaries (Psalm 106:10), and from oppression (Judges 3:31).

The New Testament vastly expands the view of salvation to one that encompasses complete deliverance from all danger that could affect our certainty of eternal life; and it teaches an eternal, physical existence in a new, perfect heaven and earth. The New Testament is explicit that salvation includes deliverance from any *penalty* (punishment) for sin and from the *power* of sin and evil. This salvation involves:

- Complete deliverance for all of eternity (2 Timothy 2:10; Hebrews 5:7-10)
- Complete spiritual deliverance from destruction (2 Corinthians 7:10; Philippians 1:28)
- Deliverance based on Jesus alone (Luke 19:10; Acts 4:12)
- Deliverance for Gentiles as well as Jews (Romans 11:11)

So the salvation that Jesus and the apostles speak of is much more than a temporary deliverance from something here on earth. And this complete salvation is a free gift, available to all people who commit themselves to Jesus as their Lord and Savior.

The commitment to embrace Jesus, which brings the wonderful gift of complete salvation, encompasses three inseparable things (see pages 16–23):

- Acceptance
- Repentance
- Lordship

Only by obtaining new life through Jesus (committing to Him) can we possibly expect to respond to God's love—by loving Him in return with all our heart, mind, soul, and strength; and loving other people in the way we love ourselves. Since God will pour out His love into our hearts by the Holy Spirit, as part of salvation (Romans 5:5), we can then go out and share His love by telling others about Jesus and the freely available gift of eternal deliverance.

Predestination and Free Will

Some people become confused over the Bible's words about "predestination" (Ephesians 1:11,12; Romans 9:16-21) and the free will of humans (Proverbs 1:28-31; Hebrews 11:24-26). They may maintain that it matters little what we do on earth because God has already decided everything beforehand. But the Bible teaches us that our actions are very important. For instance, Jesus tells His followers to "make disciples." Why would He do this if everything were already decided?

It is important to keep in mind that we can never fully understand a God who is beyond time and space (Malachi 3:6; Romans 1:20,21). God can see the beginning and end of time all at once—like seeing the whole length of a parade. He knows what we will ultimately choose—yet the choice is still ours to make. God wants us to come to know Him, and wants then to teach us character through our actions. Does it matter to us that He already knows what we will choose?

Can We Lose Eternal Salvation?

If you have committed your life to Jesus, as previously discussed, you cannot lose eternal salvation.

Once a person is truly a Christian (see pages 14–23), that person is a "new creation" in Christ (2 Corinthians 5:17). The past is gone. It is often referred to as being "born again" (John 3:3). Upon someone's being born again, the Holy Spirit takes up residence in that person, prompting him or her to become more like Christ (1 John 4:15-19).

It is important to realize that this does not mean that a person will never sin again. Quite the contrary. Development is a gradual process. But with Christ through the Holy Spirit being someone's life and source of life, that person's desires change from the old ways—selfish, evil, and prideful—to new, loving, and humble ways. The Bible refers to this outward change as "fruit" produced by the new relationship with Jesus (Galatians 5:22,23). Jesus is the "good shepherd" who cares for "His flock" of people and will never leave them (Matthew 28:20; John 10:1-18; Hebrews 13:5).

As You Choose God, He Has Chosen You

People who make a commitment to God through Jesus experience an incredible peace of mind, with joy and knowledge that God's love will protect them for eternity. (Interestingly, God already knew you would make that choice.) You may not feel a "lightning-bolt" change—few ever do. But you should feel an inner peace that is provided by the Holy Spirit, which is God's means of protecting you. It's also His means of assuring you that He is your Father, and that His gift of heaven is real (Romans 8:15-17). People who accept Jesus usually feel an overwhelming sense of love that only God can provide. Problems will still arise on earth, but Christians have a new-found strength in dealing with them. This has been attested to throughout the ages.

Christians *"fall down"* (still make mistakes), but those who have truly accepted Jesus *never fall away* from the grasp of God. As the Bible indicates, God controls salvation, not man (Jonah 2:9;

Psalm 3:8; Ephesians 2:8,9). Salvation is strictly by God's grace. It does not come through human actions (Acts 15:10,11; Galatians 2:21; Ephesians 2:4-9).

Why We Can Be Certain Salvation Is Secure

1. *The Bible clearly states so:* "I give them eternal life, and they shall never perish; *no one can snatch them out of my hand*" (Jesus, in John 10:28). "And this is the will of him who sent me, that *I shall lose none* of all that he has given me, but raise them up at the last day. For my Father's will is that everyone who looks to the Son and believes in him shall have eternal life, and I will raise him up at the last day" (Jesus, in John 6:39,40).

2. *Any assumption that we could "earn" salvation by "being good" would contradict God's grace and His declaration that we need redemption through Jesus.* The entire New Testament deals with God's love and grace, demonstrated most vividly through the death and resurrection of Jesus. Paul indicated that our continuation in God's salvation is no less dependent on Jesus than is our entrance into it. If we must "earn" something to keep our way to heaven secure, the death of Jesus was in vain (Galatians 2:21). Furthermore, since we are not capable of earning our way to heaven in the first place, we have no ability to "unearn it."

3. *Salvation based on anything but grace alone would violate God's nature.* No "good" even approaches the goodness of a perfectly holy God. This is the entire reason for Jesus' sacrifice in the first place. God's love for us does what we cannot do and provides what we cannot provide—it gives us a way to be with Him eternally in spite of our shortcomings. If we were not secure in God's gift of forgiveness, we would be in a constant, unrealistic, and ultimately despairing state of confession and repentance. Any idea that our actions "keep" our salvation would imply that dying at the "wrong moment" would mean eternal damnation, while dying at the "right moment" would send us to heaven. This would violate God's justness.

Does This Mean We Can Just Go Ahead and Sin?

No doubt some people just "go through the motions" of a statement or prayer to accept Jesus. How can these people do anything *but* continue to sin? They have no real connection with Jesus. On the other hand, those who have made a true commitment to Jesus are "new creations." They have access to His life; they can abide in Him, responding to His love by obeying His commands out of love.

Though temporary desires may cause people to sin, why would they want to *continue* to sin when they are forgiven and loved by the God of all the universe? What could be more wonderful than obeying—out of love—a God like this?

Think of an illustration. How would you feel about the enormous sacrifice of a best friend who would die—on a battlefield, perhaps—to save your life? No doubt you would feel indebted for life to such a friend. You would even feel indebted to an enemy who had done the same thing for you, and you would probably want to honor his last wishes.

Now imagine that this person was actually your worst enemy. That was our position towards Jesus (Romans 5:10). He died for everyone, including His worst enemies. Consider Him—He called those people for whom He was going to die His "friends" and asked them to obey His commands: to love others just the way He had loved them, because in doing this they would love God. As they loved others, they would tell those others about Jesus.

If you have chosen the path that has brought you to truly commit yourself to Jesus, you will return His love to others as He commanded. No one will force you to love. You will do so because you choose to. Why? Because of church rules or church peer pressure? No. You will grow in love for Jesus and His Word as a result of the Holy Spirit coming into you and demonstrating the absolute, unconditional love of God. No matter how horrible your life may have been in the past, the new life of Jesus in you will begin to show, changing your attitudes, just as promised in the Bible. Maybe not tomorrow—maybe not this year—but eventually.

Think about this—a "bad tree" gives only "bad fruit," and a "good tree" gives "good fruit" (Matthew 7:17,18). If you have been changed, you will start to produce good things ("good fruit"). Will your actions be perfect? Will you become a "religious fanatic"? No. In fact, people who follow other religions may seem "good" compared to you. The difference with Christians is that they have Jesus—they are forgiven solely by the grace of God. They don't need to earn anything. But as time goes on, the love of God will so overpower them that they will show it, whatever their past may be.

Having Assurance About Heaven

Establish a B.A.S.E. with Jesus

This is the vital step towards eternity in heaven, as has been emphasized throughout this book (see pages 14–23 for a fuller discussion). There can be no basis for assurance about getting to heaven if we do not commit to Jesus in the first place. (For ease of memory, the *Examine the Evidence* series uses the acronym B.A.S.E., which is also used by hundreds of churches around the world.)

Belief	**B**elief *that God exists and that He came to earth in the human form of Jesus Christ.*
Acceptance	**A**cceptance *of God's free forgiveness of sins through the death and resurrection of Jesus Christ.*
Repentance	**S**witching *to God's plan for your life.*
Lordship	**E**xpressly *making Jesus Christ the director of your life.*

The B.A.S.E. can be established by a simple prayer (see page 47). It's all that's necessary to get to heaven, because it's all that's necessary to come into a relationship with Jesus, if it's sincere. What does "sincere" mean? It means that you're relying on God and His power to establish your B.A.S.E., not trying to "earn" the relationship with Him by any of your own actions. He is the One who will then change your heart.

The above step ensures heaven.
Then grow with God by doing the following.

Develop a Support Program

Because of the new life of Christ within you, you will start wanting to do new things. These things will help you grow, remind you of who you now are in Christ, and give you assurance (confidence) that your entrance to heaven is secure.

Church—Meeting with other believers on a regular basis is critical. Your new life in Christ is a *shared* life—shared with God and also with other people who know Him through Jesus (Acts 2:42-47). As you live out your life and faith in the context of the church, being taught from the Bible and honoring God, you will be encouraged to keep on steadily in your everyday personal contact with God.

Christian friends—The shared life of Christ doesn't just happen during church meetings. Spend time with Christian friends in activities, small groups, and just having fun together. The Bible stresses how this mutual influence helps people ("iron sharpens iron"—Proverbs 27:17).

Education—You can build your faith by building and strengthening your belief and knowledge. The *Examine the Evidence* series can be part of this. Look also for Bible study groups and classes offered through your church and for seminars and other forms of learning about the faith.

Obedience—If you have committed yourself to Jesus, you will share His love with others as He commanded. You will want to obey Him out of love. Why? Because you have been changed. Before Jesus, you *could not* love God (or truly love anyone, for that matter). Now, God has poured out *His* love into you by the Holy Spirit (Romans 5:5).

Building Your Relationship with God

Develop Good Spiritual Habits

As mentioned in the prior pages, there are no rules to ensure heaven. Heaven is given by God's grace alone, because of our relationship with Jesus Christ as our Lord and Savior. Spiritual habits are beneficial only if they spring from a heart that has *already been changed* by God through His Holy Spirit (that is why rules and habits are useless as a means to get us to heaven). For believers, these habits demonstrate the new life and love that is now inside them, and they remind believers that God now has first place in their lives. They also help us feel assured about what we already know by faith: that we have gained heaven through Jesus and His sacrifice. And as we grow stronger in our relationship with Jesus, we will increasingly want to do things that help us. Here are some things that the Bible presents as good and helpful.

Daily Prayer—Prayer is our means of talking directly to God. Imagine that! We can talk to the Creator of the universe daily—even moment by moment—and He wants to listen! Pray daily. If you keep a "prayer journal," you'll be amazed over time how often God answers your prayers—beyond what you can even ask or think.

Reading the Bible—God communicates to Christians through the Bible because the Bible is not just a "dead book"; it is "living and active" (Hebrews 4:12). So reading the Bible daily, even a small portion, is an excellent idea. It will build your belief and faith, and God will give you direction and encouragement through it.

Giving—For the believer, the context for giving is recognizing that God has already given *us* "everything we need for life and godliness" (2 Peter 1:3). Therefore, everything we have belongs to Him, whether we use it to meet our needs, our family's needs, the needs of the church, or the needs of others. The main requirement for our giving is that it not be reluctant or "under compulsion," but willing and "cheerful," because "God loves a cheerful giver" (2 Corinthians 9:6,7). Giving generously reflects who we are as believers, and it reminds us of God's generosity to us in giving us the wonderful gift of Jesus.

Regularly Meeting with Other Believers—The practice of the early Christians (see the book of Acts) was to meet together weekly on Sunday—the most joyous day of the week, since it was the day on which Christ had risen from the dead. This has now become the tradition of nearly all of the worldwide churches. (Meeting on the Sabbath—Saturday—which was a day of rest commanded in the law of Moses, was a mark of Judaism.) Because our life in Christ is a life that is "shared" with other believers, it is a mark of our new life to be together with other Christians—for teaching, encouragement, and prayer, among other things. Meeting together helps us grow and hold onto our hope (see Hebrews 10:23-25).

Evidence of a Growing Relationship with God:

Increasing:	• Love	• Joy	• Peace
	• Patience	• Kindness	• Goodness
	• Faithfulness	• Gentleness	• Self-Control
Decreasing:	• Sexual Immorality—all kinds		• Theft
	• Greed	• Drunkenness	• Slander
	• Swindling	• Witchcraft	• Hatred
	• Discord	• Jealousy	• Fits of Rage
	• Selfishness	• Dissension	• Envy

Common Questions

Wouldn't a Loving God Allow Good People into Heaven?

Many people believe that living a good life and being kind to others is the way to heaven. Naturally, they are thinking of a "good life" in terms of our distorted human view; and such a life is far from God's standard. The Bible says that the *only* way to God in heaven is through Jesus Christ (John 14:6). So will loving and "good" people who don't accept Jesus go to hell? Yes—but how can they be truly good if they reject the love of God's Son, Jesus, who died for them?

God will allow perfectly good people into heaven. But His standard of goodness is the perfection of His Son Jesus. Hence, there is simply no other way to come to Him except through Jesus—let alone the fact that every sin of mind or body that we commit removes us further from Jesus' perfection (Matthew 5:28,29; Romans 3:22,23). Everyone is imperfect, but the good news is that God has provided Jesus as a perfect sacrifice for us. He is our way to heaven. Not accepting God's gift of love and forgiveness through Jesus, despite the Holy Spirit's prompting, is unforgivable (Mark 3:29).

How Can We Ensure the Right Relationship to Go to Heaven?

When Jesus said that not all people who use His name will enter heaven (Matthew 7:21-23), He was referring to people who think using Christ's name along with rules and rituals is the key to heaven. A *relationship* with God is not based on rituals and rules. It's based on grace, forgiveness, and on having the right standing with Him through Jesus Christ.

How to Have a Personal Relationship with God

1. B*elieve that God exists* and that He came to earth in the human form of Jesus Christ (John 3:16; Romans 10:9).
2. A*ccept God's free forgiveness* of sins and gift of new life through the death and resurrection of Jesus Christ (Ephesians 1:7-8; 2:8-10).
3. S*witch to God's plan for your life* (Ephesians 2:1-7; 1 Peter 1:21-23).
4. E*xpressly make Jesus Christ the director* of your life (Matthew 7:21-27; 1 John 4:15).

Prayer for Eternal Life with God

"Dear God, I believe You sent Your Son, Jesus, to die for my sins so I can be forgiven. I'm sorry for my sins, and I want to live the rest of my life the way You want me to. Please put Your Spirit in my life to direct me. Amen."

Then What?

People who sincerely take the above steps become members of God's family of believers. A new world of freedom and strength is available through Jesus' life within you, expressing itself through prayer and obedience to God's will. This new relationship can be strengthened by taking the following steps:

- Find a Bible-based church that you like and attend regularly.
- Set aside some time each day to pray and read the Bible.
- Locate other Christians to spend time with on a regular basis.

God's Promises to Believers
For Today
"Seek first his kingdom and his righteousness,
and all these things [things to satisfy all your needs]
will be given to you as well."
—Matthew 6:33

For Eternity
"Whoever believes in the Son has eternal life,
but whoever rejects the Son will not see life,
for God's wrath remains on him."
—John 3:36

Once we develop an eternal perspective, even the greatest problems on earth fade in significance.

Notes

Note: The author does not agree with all authors below on all viewpoints. Each reference has some findings worthy of consideration. ("Test everything"—1 Thessalonians 5:21).

1. Walvoord, John F., *The Prophecy Knowledge Handbook*, Wheaton, IL: Victor Books, 1990.
2. McDowell, Josh, and Wilson, Bill, *A Ready Defense*, San Bernardino, CA: Here's Life Publishers, Inc., 1990.
3. Muncaster, Ralph O., *How Do We Know Jesus Is God?* Eugene, OR: Harvest House, 2000.
4. Muncaster, Ralph O., *Science—Was the Bible Ahead of Its Time?* Eugene, OR: Harvest House, 2000.
5. Muncaster, Ralph O., *What Really Happens When You Die?* Eugene, OR: Harvest House, 2000.
6. Muncaster, Ralph O., *Does the Bible Predict the Future?* Eugene, OR: Harvest House, 2000.
7. Muncaster, Ralph O., *What Is the Proof for the Resurrection?* Eugene, OR: Harvest House, 2000.
8. Zodhiates, Spiros, *The Complete Word Study of the New Testament*, Chattanooga, TN: AMG Publishers, 1991.
9. Geisler, Norman, PhD, and Brooks, Ron, *When Skeptics Ask*, Grand Rapids, MI: Baker Books, 1990.
10. McDowell, Josh, *Handbook of Today's Religions*, San Bernardino, CA: Campus Crusade for Christ, 1983.
11. Ankerberg, John, and Weldon, John, *Knowing the Truth About Eternal Security*, Eugene, OR: Harvest House, 1998.

Bibliography

Archer, Gleason L., *Encyclopedia of Bible Difficulties*, Grand Rapids, MI: Zondervan Publishing House, 1982.

Basinger and Basinger, editors, *Predestination & Free Will*, Downers Grove, IL: InterVarsity Press, 1986.

Baxter, J. Sidlow, *The Other Side of Death*, Grand Rapids, MI: Kregel, 1987.

Elwell, Walter A., editor, *Evangelical Dictionary of Theology*, Grand Rapids, MI: Baker Book House, 1984.

Geisler, Norman, PhD, *Chosen But Free*, Minneapolis, MN: Bethany House Publishers, 1999.

Graham, Billy, *Death and the Life After*, Dallas, TX: Word Publishing, 1987.

Habermas, Gary R., and Moreland, J.P., *Immortality*, Nashville, TN: Nelson, 1992.

Hick, John, *Death & Eternal Life*, Louisville, KY: Westminster John Knox Press, 1994.

Life Application Bible, Wheaton, IL: Tyndale House Publishers, and Grand Rapids, MI: Zondervan Publishing House, 1991.

Smith, F. LaGard, *The Daily Bible in Chronological Order*, Eugene, OR: Harvest House, 1984.

Webster's II New Riverside University Dictionary, Riverside, CA: The Riverside Publishing Company, 1976.

Youngblood, Ronald F., *New Illustrated Bible Dictionary*, Nashville, TN: Nelson, 1995.

Zodhiates, Spiros, *The Complete Word Study of the Old Testament*, Chattanooga, TN: AMG Publishers, 1994.